QUEEN TAYS
FUNDING
TREASURE CHEST

Secure Millions In Funding For Your Business or Brand.

NATAÉ ROBINSON

Natae Robinson

Queen Tays Funding Treasure Chest

Secure Millions In Funding Fir Your Business or Brand

To those who dream of financial freedom and dare to rewrite their credit story. This book is dedicated to your resilience, commitment, and the journey toward a triumphant financial future. May these insights guide you on your path.

Natae Robinson

Contents

1.

2.

3.

4.

5.

6.

7.

8.

9.

10.

11.

12.

13.

Foreword

Welcome to a journey of financial empowerment and credit mastery! In the pages that follow, you are about to embark on a transformative exploration that goes beyond conventional financial wisdom. This book isn't just a guide; it's a roadmap to redefining your relationship with credit, unlocking funding opportunities, and orchestrating your path to financial triumph.

As a reader, you're not just flipping through words on paper; you're stepping into a realm of actionable insights, personalized strategies, and a wealth of knowledge distilled into practical steps. This book is not about one-size-fits-all solutions; it's about understanding your unique financial landscape and crafting a plan that aligns with your aspirations.

The author, Natae Robinson , a seasoned expert in media, journalism, and public relations, brings a wealth of experience to this guide. [Author's Name], also known as Queen Tay Yoncé, has dedicated her career to understanding the intricacies of credit, business funding, and financial success. Her journey, achievements, and commitment to excellence serve as an inspiration, making her the perfect guide on your path to financial empowerment.

In the chapters ahead, you'll find a meticulously structured approach, blending storytelling, actionable steps, and real-world examples. This isn't just theory; it's a playbook for transforming your financial narrative. Whether you're looking to boost your personal credit, explore business funding options, or navigate the intricate landscape of existing businesses, this book has you covered.

So, turn the page and immerse yourself in the wisdom within. Each chapter is a step closer to a financially empowered version of yourself. Take notes, absorb the insights, and, most importantly, take action. This isn't just a book; it's a catalyst for change, an invitation to elevate your financial standing, and a guide to orchestrating your own financial triumph.

Your journey begins now. Let's rewrite your financial story together.

Natae   Robinson

Preface

In the vast landscape of personal finance, the journey to financial mastery can often seem daunting. This book is born from the belief that everyone deserves access to clear, actionable guidance on navigating the intricacies of credit, business funding, and financial success.

As you delve into the pages ahead, consider this more than just a guide—it's a conversation. A conversation between you and the insights that will empower your financial decisions. From understanding credit bureaus to exploring business funding opportunities, each chapter is crafted to demystify complexities and provide you with a roadmap for progress.

Why listen to these words? Because they come from a place of experience and commitment. The author, [Author's Name], has dedicated her career to unraveling the secrets of credit, shaping narratives in media, and fostering financial success. It's a journey marked by challenges, victories, and an unwavering commitment to sharing the knowledge acquired along the way.

This book doesn't promise quick fixes; it promises guidance. It's about understanding the nuances of credit, building a solid foundation for your business, and orchestrating a financial symphony that resonates with success. It's your handbook for financial empowerment.

So, open these pages with curiosity and a willingness to take charge of your financial narrative. The insights within are not just words—they are tools for transformation. Let's embark on this journey together.

I

Part One

1

Introduction

Welcome to "Queen Tay's Funding Treasure Chest," where your journey to financial success begins! If you've ever dreamed of securing millions in funding for your business, fixing your credit, and transforming your life and business, then you've found pure gold on the internet.Are you someone aspiring to boost your personal and business credit but feel overwhelmed by the complexities of the financial world? Do you crave a comprehensive solution to not just fix your credit but also secure substantial funding for your business endeavors? Inside this treasure chest, discover step-by-step training to build your credit in 30 days, strategies for buying cash-flowing businesses, curated lists of the best business and personal trade lines, and invaluable insights on credit card stacking. This isn't just a guide; it's your road map to financial empowerment.

My name is Nataé Robinson, the powerhouse known publicly as Queen Tay Yoncé. Hailing from the vibrant streets of Harlem, NY, I have transcended boundaries in the media landscape, leaving an indelible mark as a media personality, producer, journalist, and public relations expert. My induction into FORBES The Culture in August 2020 stands as a testament to my unwavering dedication and exceptional work in the industry.As the creator of this Book, I've been where you are. I understand the challenges and frustrations that come with navigating the world of credit and funding. This book is a culmination of my experiences, learning, and the proven strategies that have transformed my own life and business.

Beyond my thriving career, I specializes in monetizing brands, offering invaluable insights and assistance to celebrities and businesses. My strategic approach has contributed to fundraising efforts exceeding $120 Million for the water crisis in Newark, NJ.Rest assured, the information within this bundle is not theoretical—it's a compilation of practical steps that have yielded results. Your journey is backed by proven methods, ensuring that your investment in yourself will pay off.Transform your credit profile, secure substantial funding, and embark on a path to financial success. The benefits extend beyond just your business; they touch every aspect of your life.

This isn't a promise without substance. The strategies outlined have helped numerous individuals like yourself achieve financial success. Realize the potential by following the path laid out in this bundle.I promise you more than just financial transformation; I promise a paradigm shift in the way you approach credit, funding, and business. Your success story begins with the commitment to follow this guide diligently.The time for financial transformation is now. Delaying your journey only postpones the benefits you could be reaping. Don't let opportunities slip away; act on your aspirations today.Turn the page and embark on a transformative journey. Your success awaits within "Queen Tay's Funding Treasure Chest." Start building your credit, securing funding, and transforming your life and business. Don't just read—act!

2

Unlocking Credit Power

Believe in Your Credit Success!

Embark on a journey where your credit becomes the key to unlocking financial success. Let me share a real-life story that mirrors the challenges many face when beginning this transformative process.

1. **Mastering Your Personal Credit Score :** Explore the best credit repair tools and strategies included in this book, your inaugural stride on the path to credit mastery.

2. **Turbocharge with Personal Tradelines :** Learn how to amplify your credit score by strategically incorporating personal tradelines. These steps set the stage for forthcoming credit card applications and funding opportunities.

3. **Business Owners' Blueprint :** Entrepreneurs, follow a parallel process for your business credit journey. Leverage the recommended tradelines, boost your business credit score, and confidently apply for funding.

4. **Navigating the Credit Inquiry Maze :** Discover the importance of minimizing credit inquiries. Delve into the next page to understand which banks pull from specific credit bureaus—a crucial strategy known as "stacking."

5. **Unlocking Business Ownership :** For those eyeing business ownership, find guidance on purchasing existing businesses that generate monthly cash flow. Follow the directions provided and step into entrepreneurship seamlessly.

Believe in the potential of your credit journey. Implement these five steps diligently, and witness the transformation in your personal and business finances. Your journey to financial success is marked by intentional steps, each bringing you closer to your goals.

3

Navigating Credit Inquiries

Taking Control of Your Credit Destiny!

Before delving into this chapter, remember the crucial steps you've taken in unlocking your personal credit power. These actions are the building blocks of your financial success.As we venture into the intricacies of credit inquiries, let me share a story that underscores the significance of understanding how different banks approach credit checks.

Understanding Equifax-Centric Banks

Navigating the landscape of credit evaluation is crucial in your journey to financial empowerment. This chapter unveils the list of banks that rely on Equifax for credit checks, providing you with essential insights into their practices and how they influence your credit profile.

From reputable institutions like PenFed to major players like Wells Fargo, each bank's credit evaluation methods vary. Understanding these nuances is key to deciphering the impact on your creditworthiness. Equifax, as one of the major credit bureaus, plays a pivotal role in shaping your credit narrative.

Knowing which banks pull from Equifax arms you with a strategic advantage. It's not just about information; it's about empowerment. The power to make informed decisions that safeguard your credit score and financial future. This awareness serves as your compass in the credit landscape, allowing you to navigate it with confidence.

As you delve into the details of Equifax-centric banks, consider the broader context of your credit journey. Each piece of information is a puzzle, and by understanding how these banks operate, you gain a clearer picture of your credit profile. Let's embark on this exploration together, unlocking the knowledge that propels you toward credit mastery.

The Power of Knowledge in Credit Checks

In the realm of credit, knowledge is more than power; it's your shield against financial pitfalls. This section dives deep into the significance of understanding which banks pull credit checks from Equifax. This knowledge becomes your armor, fortifying your credit profile against unnecessary hits.

Credit checks are the gatekeepers to your financial opportunities. The more you know about them, the better equipped you are to make strategic decisions. Equifax, being a major credit bureau, holds a substantial influence on your creditworthiness. Armed with this awareness, you transform from a passive participant to an active navigator of your credit destiny.

Empowerment lies in informed choices, especially when it comes to managing credit inquiries. This chapter unveils the power of knowledge in guiding your actions. It's not just about knowing; it's about using that knowledge to your advantage. As you absorb this information, envision it as a tool that shapes your credit landscape in a way that aligns with your financial goals.

Your journey to financial success requires more than mere awareness; it demands an understanding of how to leverage that awareness. Knowledge, when applied strategically, becomes a force multiplier in your credit journey. Let's harness that power and elevate your credit game to new heights.

Crafting Your Credit Inquiry Strategy

In the intricate world of credit, crafting a personalized strategy is your key to success. This section provides you with the tools and insights needed to navigate the credit inquiry maze effectively. Your credit profile is not just a record; it's a narrative, and you have the power to craft it thoughtfully.

Understanding the nuances of credit checks from Equifax is the first step in your strategic approach. Armed with this knowledge, you're ready to design a credit inquiry strategy that aligns with your financial objectives. It's not about avoiding credit checks; it's about orchestrating them in a way that enhances, rather than diminishes, your creditworthiness.

Your personalized strategy involves more than just minimizing inquiries; it's about showcasing your creditworthiness to potential lenders. This chapter guides you through the steps of crafting a strategy that not only protects your credit score but also positions you as a desirable candidate for financial opportunities.

As you embark on this journey of crafting your credit inquiry strategy, consider it a transformative process. You're not just learning; you're evolving into a credit-savvy individual who navigates the credit landscape with purpose. Let's embark on this strategic journey together, creating a credit narrative that opens doors to your financial aspirations.

EQUIFAX

- PenFed
- Citibank
- Truist
- SECU of MD
- FCU
- Keybank
- AG Fed
- AOD XR
- Justice FCU
- DCU
- PNC
- NIH FCU
- Langley
- Sky Point FCU
- BOA
- Chevron
- Credit Union of TX
- One Main Financial
- Citizens Bank
- Wells Fargo
- USAA
- Digital CU
- Community First Bank Credit Union
- NRLF CU
- Elan

Congratulations on uncovering the banks tied to Equifax inquiries. Take actionable steps to apply this knowledge in real life—craft your personalized credit inquiry strategy. Remember, informed decisions today lead to a stronger financial future tomorrow.

4

Navigating Experian's Credit Waters

Charting Your Course Through Experian's Realm!

Before embarking on the Experian journey, reflect on the Equifax insights you've gained. These insights are your foundation as you delve into the nuances of Experian-related credit checks.As we navigate the realm of Experian, consider this chapter a guiding beacon through the credit waters. Let me share a story to emphasize the importance of maintaining focus, especially when tackling new information.

Decoding Experian-Centric Banks

Embark on a journey through the intricacies of credit evaluations as we decode the list of banks relying on Experian for this crucial process. From industry giants like Discover to financial institutions like FNBO, understanding their credit evaluation practices is essential for shaping your credit profile and influencing lending opportunities.

Experian, as a major credit bureau, plays a pivotal role in determining your creditworthiness. Each bank on the list brings its unique approach to credit evaluations, impacting how they perceive and assess your financial reliability. By decoding the practices of Experian-centric banks, you gain insights that go beyond mere information – you gain the power to strategically navigate the credit landscape.

As you delve into the details of Experian-centric banks, consider the broader context of your credit journey. Knowledge is not just about awareness; it's about wielding that awareness to your advantage. Together, let's unravel the complexities, decoding the language of credit evaluations and transforming it into a roadmap for your financial success.

Staying Focused Amidst Learning Challenges

Navigating the terrain of credit mastery can be challenging, and it's essential to acknowledge the potential hurdles that readers might face in grasping new information. Learning challenges are a natural part of the journey, and recognizing them is the first step toward overcoming them.

In this section, we introduce strategies to help readers stay focused amid challenges. Whether it's the complexity of credit evaluations or the intricacies of financial terms, staying engaged is key. We emphasize the importance of pacing oneself, breaking down complex information into manageable chunks, and celebrating small victories along the way.

As part of our commitment to your success, we also introduce a free tool or template to support your learning journey. This resource is designed to simplify complex concepts, providing a structured approach to credit mastery. Remember, every challenge you encounter is an opportunity for growth, and with the right strategies and tools, you can navigate the learning process with confidence.

Leveraging Free Tools for Credit Mastery

In the quest for credit mastery, practical tools become your allies. This section introduces a valuable free tool or template crafted to assist readers in navigating Experian-related credit inquiries. Our goal is to empower you with resources that not only simplify the learning process but also keep you on track toward credit proficiency.

Leveraging free tools is a strategic approach to credit mastery. It's about more than just acquiring knowledge; it's about applying that knowledge in a way that transforms it into a practical skill. The introduced tool or template serves as a guide, aligning with the content you've explored and providing a hands-on experience that reinforces your understanding of Experian-centric credit evaluations.

As you explore this section, envision these tools as companions on your journey to credit mastery. Together, let's leverage these resources to demystify credit inquiries, enhance your understanding of Experian's role, and ultimately, empower you to take control of your financial narrative.

EXPERIAN

- Discover Chase
- AMEX
- TD Bank
- PNC Bank Citibank
- AM Trust Fidelity
- PSECU
- NASA FOU
- Ist Tech FCU
- Andrews FCU
- State Dept FCU
- Mission Lane
- FNBO

As you navigate the Experian credit waters, remember the Equifax lessons and stay focused on the journey. Leverage the introduced free tools to streamline your understanding. Your key takeaway: gradual progress leads to credit mastery.

5

Transunion Triumphs

Celebrating Your Progress with Transunion!

Take a moment to bask in your achievements so far, navigating Equifax and Experian's territories. Your journey is a testament to your commitment and progress.As we venture into the Transunion chapter, let me applaud your dedication. Consider this a celebration of your journey, and let me share a story that mirrors your determination.

Mastering Transunion-Centric Banks

Embark on a comprehensive exploration of credit evaluations as we delve into the list of banks relying on TransUnion for this critical process. From Applied Bank to Synchrony, each institution's credit evaluation practices have a unique impact on your credit profile and the financial opportunities available to you.

TransUnion, as a major credit bureau, plays a pivotal role in shaping your credit narrative. Understanding how each bank on this list utilizes TransUnion's data is a strategic move toward credit mastery. These insights go beyond surface-level information; they empower you to navigate the intricacies of credit evaluations with a nuanced understanding.

As you navigate through the details of TransUnion-centric banks, consider the broader context of your credit journey. This chapter is not just about acquiring information; it's about gaining mastery over your credit profile. Together, let's unravel the complexities, mastering the language of TransUnion-centric credit evaluations and leveraging this knowledge for financial empowerment.

Commending Your Progress

A moment of celebration is in order. Commend yourself for the dedication and quick wins you've achieved on your credit mastery journey. Recognizing your progress is not just a formality; it's an essential step in fostering motivation and a sense of accomplishment.

Your commitment to understanding credit evaluations from major bureaus like TransUnion is commendable. Quick wins signify more than just small achievements; they symbolize the proactive steps you've taken toward financial empowerment. This acknowledgment is a testament to your dedication and a reminder that every step forward, no matter how small, is a victory in your credit mastery journey.

As you reflect on your progress, consider this moment as a stepping stone toward greater financial proficiency. Your journey doesn't end here; it's an ongoing exploration of credit nuances and financial strategies. Take pride in your accomplishments, and let this recognition fuel your motivation for the next steps in your credit mastery journey.

Next Steps in Your Credit Mastery Journey

Guiding you through the next steps in your credit mastery journey is a pivotal aspect of our commitment to your success. Having delved into the intricacies of TransUnion-centric banks, it's time to consider what comes next in your pursuit of credit proficiency.

This chapter subtly introduces the idea of progressing to the next level in your credit mastery journey. It's an invitation to explore additional resources that can further support you in understanding credit evaluations, financial strategies, and advanced concepts. Consider it a roadmap for continuous learning, with each step bringing you closer to a heightened level of credit expertise.

The next steps are not just about acquiring more information; they're about refining your mastery and deepening your understanding. Whether it's advanced credit concepts, financial planning strategies, or niche topics within credit management, the journey continues. Let's chart these next steps together, ensuring your path to credit mastery is not only educational but also fulfilling and empowering.

TRANSUNION

- Applied Bank

- Barclays
- 5th 3rd Bank Merrick Bank
- BBVA
- US Bank
- CFNA
- Univest
- Ist Premier Bank
- Alliant CU
- Navy Federal
- Apple FCU
- Tower FCU
- Southwest
- Truemark Fin Synchrony

Congratulations on conquering Transunion's domain! Reflect on your journey, appreciate your progress, and consider how further resources can enhance your credit mastery. Your key takeaway: every step forward is a step toward financial empowerment.

6

Personal Credit Symphony with Tradelines

Harmonizing Your Personal Credit Journey!

Before diving into the realm of personal credit tradelines, reflect on your victories with personal credit and the valuable lessons from navigating Equifax, Experian, and Transunion. Your journey is uniquely yours, and each step is a foundation for the next.

As we delve into the art of building personal credit with tradelines, envision it as the crescendo of your financial symphony. Let me share stories that illuminate the transformative power of personal credit journeys.

Embracing the Power of Personal Tradelines

Embark on a journey of financial transformation by delving into the profound impact of personal tradelines. These financial instruments hold the key to enhancing your credit melody, creating harmonies that resonate throughout your credit profile and open doors to new financial opportunities.

Personal tradelines are not merely entries on your credit report; they are musical notes that compose the intricate melody of your creditworthiness. Understanding their power is the first step in orchestrating a credit symphony that reflects your financial responsibility and stability.

As you embrace the power of personal tradelines, envision them as the instrumental elements in the composition of your credit story. Each tradeline contributes to the overall harmony, shaping the narrative that lenders perceive. Together, let's explore the transformative potential of personal tradelines and unlock the symphony of financial opportunities they can bring.

Strategically Incorporating Personal Tradelines

Navigating the world of personal tradelines requires strategic acumen. In this section, we embark on the process of selecting and incorporating these financial instruments with precision. Uncover the nuances and intricacies involved, ensuring that each chosen tradeline contributes strategically to the harmonious composition of your personal credit.

Selecting personal tradelines is akin to curating a playlist for your credit journey. Each tradeline has its unique contribution to the melody, whether it's enhancing credit diversity, extending credit history, or increasing credit limits. This section provides you with the insights needed to make informed decisions, strategically incorporating tradelines that align with your financial goals.

Consider this part of the journey as a symphony conductor, strategically placing each instrument to create a masterpiece. Your credit profile is the composition, and each tradeline is a note that plays a vital role. Let's navigate this process together, ensuring that your credit symphony resonates with financial harmony.

Orchestrating Your Personal Credit Symphony

The final steps in your journey involve orchestrating your personal credit symphony. Learn how to nurture and maintain your credit profile, ensuring it plays a melodious tune that attracts favorable financial opportunities. This section provides the essential insights to keep your credit symphony in harmony, resonating positively with potential lenders and financial institutions.

Maintaining a well-orchestrated credit symphony involves regular care and attention. This section guides you through the practices of responsible credit management, emphasizing the importance of timely payments, monitoring your credit report, and addressing any discrepancies promptly. Your personal credit symphony is a dynamic composition, and orchestrating it effectively ensures its continued resonance.

Consider this chapter as the crescendo in your credit journey—the culmination of strategic decisions, informed choices, and financial responsibility. As you navigate the final steps, envision your credit profile as a symphony that reflects your financial prowess and invites opportunities with its harmonious melody.

BUILD YOUR PERSONAL CREDIT EASY WITH TRADELINES

- SELF Lender
- Ava
- Kickoff
- Credit Strong
- StellarFi Cushion Cheese
- Kovo SeedFi
- Extra Card
- Boom
- Rental Kharma
- Brigit
- Grow Credit
- Experian Boost

Reflect on your victories, absorb the insights on personal credit tradelines, and envision the symphony of success your personal credit can achieve. Take actionable steps to incorporate and nurture your personal tradelines, turning your financial vision into reality. Your key takeaway: your personal credit symphony begins with the strategic placement of tradeline instruments.

7

Elevating Your Business with Tradelines

Crafting Your Business Credit Symphony!

Before embarking on the final leg of your credit journey, revisit the victories with Personal credit tradelines. Each step has brought you closer to financial empowerment, and the symphony of success is within reach.As we explore the world of business credit, envision it as the crescendo of your financial symphony. Allow me to share a story that captures the essence of turning business credit into a harmonious melody.

Initiating Business Credit Building

Embark on the exciting journey of building your business credit by delving into the significance of tradelines. In the world of business finance, tradelines play a crucial role in shaping the credit foundation of your enterprise. Understanding their impact is the first step toward establishing a robust credit profile that opens doors to financial opportunities.

Tradelines for your business are more than just entries on a credit report; they are the building blocks of a strong credit foundation. This section initiates your exploration into the transformative power of business tradelines, highlighting how they contribute to the symphony of your business credit. Envision this journey as a musical composition where each tradeline plays a distinctive note, creating a harmonious credit melody for your business.

As we initiate the business credit building process, recognize the potential for financial growth and stability that lies ahead. Tradelines are the instruments that set the tone for your business credit journey, and understanding their significance is the key to orchestrating a successful financial future for your enterprise.

Strategically Selecting Business Tradelines

In the intricate landscape of business credit, selecting the right tradelines is a strategic endeavor. This section guides you through the process of strategically choosing business tradelines that align with your financial goals. Explore the nuances involved in this selection process, understanding how each tradeline contributes to the symphony of your business credit profile.

Strategic selection of business tradelines involves more than just adding entries to your credit report; it's about curating a composition that reflects the financial stability and credibility of your business. Consider this part of the journey as the conductor orchestrating the business credit symphony. Each tradeline represents an instrument that plays a unique role in creating a harmonious credit profile for your enterprise.

As you navigate the complexities of business credit building, envision each tradeline as a musical note contributing to the overall melody. This section provides insights into making informed choices, ensuring that the tradelines you select harmonize with the financial narrative you aim to create for your business.

Nurturing Your Business Credit Symphony

The journey of building business credit extends beyond initiation – it involves the ongoing process of nurturing and maintaining your business credit symphony. Dive into the strategies for leveraging tradelines as instruments that play a harmonious tune, attracting opportunities and fostering financial success for your enterprise.

Nurturing your business credit involves proactive measures to ensure the continued resonance of your credit symphony. Discover the practices of responsible credit management, timely payments, and monitoring your business credit report. Tradelines are not static entries; they are dynamic instruments that require care and attention to maintain their positive impact on your business credit profile.

Consider this section as the guide to nurturing a thriving business credit symphony. Learn how to keep your credit profile in tune with your financial goals, attracting favorable opportunities and establishing your business as a credible player in the financial landscape. As you nurture your business credit, envision the ongoing success and growth that accompanies a harmonious credit melody for your enterprise.

BUILD YOUR BUSINESS CREDIT EASY WITH TRADELINES

- Credit Strong Business
- Grow Credit
- NAV Boost eCredible
- Uline Quill
- Grainger
- Crown Office Supplies Summa Office Supplies
- Fuel Cards

Reflect on your journey, absorb the insights on business credit tradelines, and envision the symphony of success your business can achieve. Take actionable steps to select and nurture your tradelines, turning your vision into a reality. Your key takeaway: your business credit symphony begins with the strategic placement of tradeline instruments.

8

Unveiling No PG Business Lenders

Unlocking the Gateway to No Personal Guarantee Business Loans!

As you stand on the threshold of discovering lenders offering no personal guarantee business loans, reflect on the impactful journey—from building personal and business credit to orchestrating a financial symphony. Your readiness to explore this final chapter signals a step toward financial autonomy.Imagine a business landscape where your success doesn't hinge on personal guarantees. Let me share a story that encapsulates the transformative power of accessing business funding without compromising your personal assets.

Navigating the No PG Business Lenders Landscape

Embark on a journey of financial autonomy as we explore the comprehensive list of no personal guarantee (PG) business lenders in the United States. This resource serves as your indispensable guide to securing funding without the encumbrance of personal guarantees, offering you a landscape of possibilities for your business ventures.

Understanding the terrain of no PG business lenders is akin to navigating uncharted waters. This section provides you with a detailed map, outlining lenders who recognize the potential of your business without requiring personal guarantees. Each lender on this list becomes a waypoint on your financial journey, offering a path toward securing funding without compromising personal assets.

Consider this exploration as a strategic move toward financial empowerment. The landscape of no PG business lenders is rich with opportunities for businesses seeking funding avenues that prioritize the enterprise's potential rather than personal assurances. Let's navigate this landscape together, unlocking doors to financial independence and success.

Strategic Approaches to Secure No PG Business Funding

In the dynamic world of business funding, securing capital without personal guarantees requires strategic finesse. This section unveils the intricacies of no PG business funding, offering insights into strategic approaches that increase your chances of success. Navigate this unique funding landscape armed with the knowledge and best practices that empower you on your quest for financial support.

Understanding the nuances of approaching no PG business funding is crucial. It's not just about identifying lenders but also about crafting a compelling narrative for your business. Learn the art of presenting your business in a way that resonates with these lenders, showcasing its potential and minimizing their perceived risks. This strategic approach positions you as a credible candidate in the competitive arena of business funding.

Consider this section as your strategic playbook for securing no PG business funding. By mastering these approaches, you enhance your ability to navigate the landscape with confidence, increasing the likelihood of obtaining the financial support your business needs. Let's delve into the strategies that elevate your business's appeal in the eyes of no PG lenders, paving the way for funding success.

Expanding Your Financial Horizon

As you explore the realm of no PG business lenders, consider ways to expand your financial horizon beyond the confines of personal guarantees. This section invites you to broaden your perspective and discover additional resources, networks, or strategies that complement your journey toward financial autonomy.

Expanding your financial horizon is not just about accessing funds; it's about embracing a holistic approach to financial independence. Look beyond traditional avenues and explore networks that align with your business goals. Consider alternative strategies that provide flexibility and empower your business to thrive without the burden of personal guarantees.

This section serves as a gateway to a broader financial landscape, offering ideas and possibilities that extend beyond conventional routes. By expanding your financial horizon, you position your business to harness diverse opportunities and navigate the ever-evolving financial terrain with resilience and adaptability. Let's embark on this journey together, opening doors to a more expansive and dynamic financial future for your enterprise.

NO PERSONAL GUARANTEE (PG) BUSINESS LENDERS IN THE USA

- OnDeck
- Fundbox
- Brex
- Kabbage
- Divvy
- Stripe Card
- Sams Club Business Card Shell Small Business Card
- Office Depot Business Credit Card Silicon Valley Bank Innovators Card
- Staples More Card
- Coast
- Bento
- Charity Charger Non-Profit Business Card

Empower yourself with the knowledge of no personal guarantee business lenders. Take action by exploring the list provided and strategically approaching your funding endeavors. Your key takeaway: financial autonomy is within reach, and these steps will guide you to unlock the gateway.

9

Unleashing Business Funding Opportunities

Embarking on a Journey to Business Funding Success!

As you stand on the brink of exploring diverse business funding opportunities, recall the strides you've made—from understanding credit nuances to uncovering lenders offering no personal guarantee loans. Each step has been a pivotal moment leading you to this chapter, poised for business funding success.Picture a realm where your business aspirations are fueled by a diverse range of funding sources. Let me weave a narrative that captures the essence of unlocking the doors to expansive business funding possibilities.

Navigating the Business Funding Landscape

Embark on a transformative journey through the expansive terrain of business funding. This section serves as your comprehensive guide, unveiling a diverse and rich list of general business funding opportunities available for your entrepreneurial ventures. As you navigate this landscape, each funding option becomes a potential catalyst for the growth and success of your business.

The business funding landscape is akin to a vast and varied ecosystem, each funding source representing a unique ecosystem niche. From traditional loans to innovative funding models, this guide offers you a panoramic view of the opportunities that await your business. Consider this section as your roadmap, guiding you through the intricacies of securing the financial support your business needs to thrive.

Delve into the details of each funding option, understanding their nuances and potential implications for your business. This journey is not just about finding funding; it's about aligning your business with the right financial resources that resonate with your goals and aspirations. Let's embark on this enlightening journey, exploring the vast possibilities that the business funding landscape has to offer.

Strategic Approaches to Secure Business Funding

In the dynamic and competitive arena of business funding, strategic approaches are paramount. This section dives deep into the intricacies of securing business funding, providing you with key insights and best practices to enhance your ability to navigate this intricate landscape successfully. By adopting strategic approaches, you position your business as a strong and attractive candidate for financial support.

Understanding the dynamics of business funding is not just about identifying sources but also about crafting a compelling narrative for your business. Learn how to present your business in a way that resonates with potential funders, showcasing its unique value proposition and potential for growth. This strategic mindset transforms the process of securing funding into a purposeful journey, where each step aligns with your business objectives.

Consider this section as your strategic playbook for the business funding game. Whether you're exploring traditional lenders, venture capital, or alternative funding models, strategic approaches guide you through the complexities, increasing your chances of success. Let's delve into the strategies that empower your business to secure the funding it needs to thrive and prosper.

Expanding Your Business Financial Arsenal

As you navigate the business funding landscape, consider ways to expand your business financial arsenal beyond conventional sources. This section encourages you to explore additional funding options, networks, or innovative strategies that can elevate your business funding game to new heights.

Think of your business financial arsenal as a dynamic toolkit, where each funding source adds a valuable instrument. Beyond traditional loans, venture capital, or angel investors, there exist untapped opportunities that can contribute to your business's financial resilience. This section serves as a catalyst for creative thinking, prompting you to explore unconventional avenues and networks that align with your business goals.

By expanding your business financial arsenal, you empower your business with versatility and adaptability in the ever-evolving financial landscape. Consider this section as an invitation to think outside the box, embracing diverse funding options that resonate with your business vision. Let's explore innovative strategies and resources together, enhancing your business's financial strength and paving the way for sustained success.

BUSINESS FUNDING

- OnDeck
- Fundbox Kabbage Lendio
- Biz2Credit
- National Business Capital
- Gokapital
- Commercial Loan Direct
- Funding Circle
- Upstart
- Fundera Prosper
- Big Think Capital
- ROK Financial LendingTree
- Credibly SBA.gov
- National Funding
- Torro Business Funding
- Rapid Finance
- Uplyft
- Bluevine
- David Allen Capital (FAST APPROVALS)

Equip yourself with the knowledge of diverse business funding opportunities. Take action by exploring the comprehensive list provided and strategically approaching your funding endeavors. Your key takeaway: a world of business funding possibilities awaits, and these steps will guide you to unleash your business's full financial potential.As you conclude this chapter, anticipate the clear next steps awaiting you in the final chapter. Your journey is on the cusp of reaching new heights, and I'm thrilled to guide you toward unparalleled success in   business   funding.

10

Seizing Profitable Ventures - Buying Cashflowing Businesses

Your Gateway to Financial Prosperity - Acquiring Profitable Enterprises!

As you stand at the precipice of a transformative decision—buying an existing, cashflowing business—reflect on the journey traversed. From credit mastery to exploring diverse funding sources, each step has been a strategic move leading you to this pivotal chapter.Imagine stepping into a business that's already flourishing, where cash is flowing and opportunities abound. Allow me to share a story that encapsulates the incredible potential of acquiring a business that's already making waves.

Navigating the Landscape of Existing Businesses

Delve into the mini-steps that form the strategic foundation of acquiring a cash-flowing business. This section provides a comprehensive exploration of the intricacies involved in strategically acquiring an existing business, ensuring you are well-equipped to navigate the complexities of this venture.

The process of acquiring a business is akin to a delicate dance, where each step requires precision and strategic thinking. Uncover key considerations in evaluating potential businesses, negotiating favorable terms, and conducting due diligence that goes beyond the surface. This section acts as your guide, offering insights into the art of strategic business acquisition, empowering you to make decisions that align with your business goals.

Consider the negotiation table not just as a transactional space but as a strategic arena where your vision and the business's potential converge. Understand the nuances of due diligence, ensuring a thorough examination of the business's financial health and operational aspects. By mastering these mini-steps, you elevate your ability to strategically acquire a business with confidence, setting the stage for a successful venture.

Strategic Steps in the Business Acquisition Process

Chart your unique path to financial prosperity by taking the next steps in acquiring a business that aligns with your goals and aspirations. This section invites you to explore ways to capitalize on the opportunity presented by acquiring an existing business, ensuring a smooth transition into business ownership and financial success.

As you embark on this path, envision each step as a milestone toward financial prosperity. Explore strategies to optimize the acquired business, identify growth opportunities, and position yourself as a successful business owner. Whether you are a seasoned entrepreneur or venturing into business ownership for the first time, this section serves as your guide to charting a course toward financial prosperity through strategic business acquisition.

Consider this part of the journey as an investment in your future, where the acquisition of a cash-flowing business becomes a catalyst for financial success. Explore the possibilities, capitalize on the opportunities, and take deliberate steps toward securing your path to financial prosperity through strategic business ownership.

Your Path to Financial Prosperity

Chart your unique path to financial prosperity by taking the next steps in acquiring a business that aligns with your goals and aspirations. This section invites you to explore ways to capitalize on the opportunity presented by acquiring an existing business, ensuring a smooth transition into business ownership and financial success.

As you embark on this path, envision each step as a milestone toward financial prosperity. Explore strategies to optimize the acquired business, identify growth opportunities, and position yourself as a successful business owner. Whether you are a seasoned entrepreneur or venturing into business ownership for the first time, this section serves as your guide to charting a course toward financial prosperity through strategic business acquisition.

Consider this part of the journey as an investment in your future, where the acquisition of a cash-flowing business becomes a catalyst for financial success. Explore the possibilities, capitalize on the opportunities, and take deliberate steps toward securing your path to financial prosperity through strategic business ownership.

BUY AN EXISTING BUSINESS THAT'S ALREADY CASHFLOWING

- BizBuySell
- Acquire
- Flippa.com
- Nano Flips
- Tiny Aquistions
- Empire Flippers
- E-Commerce Flipper
- Micro Acquire
- Quiet Light
- FE International

Seize the potential of acquiring a cashflowing business. Take action by exploring websites and platforms, understanding the acquisition process, and initiating steps toward financial prosperity. Your key takeaway: your journey to business ownership and financial success begins with informed decisions and strategic moves.

11

Charting Your Financial Triumph

Your Journey to Financial Triumph Awaits!

As you stand at the culmination of this transformative journey, take a moment to reflect on the wealth of knowledge gained—from navigating personal and business credit to discovering strategic tradelines. Your journey is a testament to your dedication, and the symphony of financial success is ready to play.

Charting Your Financial Triumph

As you stand at the threshold of financial transformation, fueled by the knowledge gained from this guide, it's time to forge ahead with confidence and purpose. The journey you've embarked upon is not just a chapter in a book but a profound shift towards a brighter financial future. Let's conclude this empowering exploration with personalized steps tailored to your individual path.

Your Customized Action Plan:

Instead of a standardized 30-day challenge, I encourage you to create a personalized action plan. Reflect on the strategies resonating most with your goals and circumstances. Outline specific, achievable steps for the coming weeks that align with your unique financial aspirations. This isn't a one-size-fits-all approach; it's about crafting a roadmap that suits your journey.

Your Continued Journey

As you move forward, remember that financial triumph is a continuous journey, not bound by a specific timeframe. Embrace each step with intention and celebrate every achievement along the way. Stay attuned to your evolving goals, adjusting your action plan as needed. Your journey is unique, and your progress is a testament to your commitment.

This isn't a conclusion but an invitation—to persist in your financial growth, adapting strategies to fit your needs. The power lies in your hands, and as you navigate your customized action plan, you're not just charting a course to financial triumph; you're crafting a legacy of financial empowerment that's uniquely yours.

33